E... AND AGAPE

RANIERO CANTALAMESSA

# EROS AND AGAPE
## The two sides of love

*Translated by Liam Kelly*

ST PAULS

Cover design: DX Imaging

ST PAULS Publishing
187 Battersea Bridge Road, London SW11 3AS, UK
www.stpaulspublishing.com

Copyright © 2012 ST PAULS-UK
Translated from the Italian original *Eros e Agape*
© Edizioni San Paolo s.r.l. – Cinisello Balsamo (MI)

ISBN: 978-0-85439-830-0

A catalogue record is available
for this book from the British Library.

Set by C. González, ssp.
Printed by Melita Press, Malta

ST PAULS is an activity of the priests and brothers
of the Society of St Paul who proclaim the Gospel
through the media of social communication.

# CONTENTS

PREFACE 7

I. CHRISTIAN LOVE:
   A PEARL BETWEEN TWO SHELLS 9

   1. Cool or hot jazz? 9
   2. The incompatibility of the two loves? 12
   3. Return to the synthesis 17
   4. Christ, primary object
      of the human eros 21

II. GOD ALSO DESIRES MAN 29

   1. The love of God in eternity 30
   2. The love of God in creation 33
   3. The love of God in revelation 35
   4. The love of God in the incarnation 37
   5. If this is not love… 39
   6. We have believed in the love of God! 41

III. LET CHARITY BE WITHOUT PRETENCE    47

    1. Love your neighbour as yourself    47
    2. Love each other with a sincere heart    53
    3. Love edifies    59

IV. AN EFFECTIVE LOVE: THE SOCIAL SIGNIFICANCE OF THE GOSPEL    65

    1. The exercise of charity    65
    2. The emergence of the social problem    67
    3. Theological reflection: Liberal and dialectical theology    71
    4. The Church's social doctrine    77
    5. To serve, and not be served    81

V. HE LOVED US WHEN WE WERE ENEMIES: GOOD FRIDAY HOMILY    85

# PREFACE

THIS book contains the Lent 2011 meditations given to the Papal Household, in the presence of Pope Benedict XVI and members of the Papal Chapel. Only exceptionally, when it was impossible to do otherwise without losing the strength and meaning of a phrase, have I retained the references to that specific spoken occasion.

In the wake of Benedict XVI's two encyclicals devoted to the theme of charity *(Deus caritas est* and *Caritas in veritate),* the aim has been to begin from the ultimate source of love which is God, in order to highlight the beauty of the Christian ideal which reconciles in itself eros and agape and the need for all human relations to be imbued with it.

Particular attention is dedicated to the qualities with which, according to the New

Testament, love must be clothed. It must be a "sincere" love, without hypocrisy, but also "effective", not consisting simply in sentiments and words, but in concrete gestures with regard to others. In short, a love which starts from the heart but passes through the hands! Along this line of thought lies the reflection developing the social significance of the Gospel.

The last chapter, dedicated to the love "of which there is none greater", that of Christ on the cross, reproduces the homily given the same year during the Liturgy of the Passion held in St Peter's Basilica.

# I

# CHRISTIAN LOVE: A PEARL BETWEEN TWO SHELLS

### 1. Cool or hot jazz?

THERE IS an area in which secularisation acts in a particularly widespread and ominous manner, and that is the area of love. The secularisation of love consists in separating human love, in all its forms, from God, reducing it to something purely "profane", where God is "in the way", or is even a nuisance.

The theme of love is important not just for evangelisation, that is, relations with the world; it is also, and first of all, important for the inner life of the Church, for the sanctification of its members. This is the perspective in which Benedict XVI's encyclical *Deus caritas* est lies and in which I am placing these reflections, too.

Love suffers from a tragic separation not just in the mind-set of the secularised world, but also, on the opposite side, among believers and especially among consecrated souls. In very simplistic terms, we can express the situation thus: in the world we find eros without agape; among believers we often find agape without eros.

Eros without agape is a romantic love, more often passionate, even to the point of violence. A love of conquest, which fatally reduces the other person to an object of one's own pleasure and ignores every dimension of sacrifice, faithfulness and self-giving. There is no need to keep on describing this love because it is a reality which is in front of our eyes every day, advertised in a hammering way by novels, films, TV fiction, the internet, and gossip magazines. It is what common language now means by the word "love".

For us it is more useful to understand what is meant by agape without eros. In music there is a distinction which can help us to have some idea of it: that between hot and cool jazz. Somewhere I read this characterisation of the two genres, although I know it is not the only distinction possible. *Hot* jazz is passionate jazz, vigorous, expressive, made up of outbursts, feelings and therefore original surges and improvisations. *Cool* jazz is what happens with the move to professionalism: the feelings become repetitive, inspiration is replaced by technique, spontaneity by virtuosity, and one works more with the head than the heart.

According to this distinction, agape without eros seems to us to be like "cold love", "love that is only skin deep", more by the dictation of will than the intimate impulse of the heart; a falling into a pre-constituted mould, rather than creating one's own unique one, just as every human being is unique before God. The actions of love addressed to God are similar, in this case, to those of innocent people in love who write love letters copied from a special handbook.

If worldly love is a body without a soul, religious love practised in this way is a soul without a body. The human being is not an angel, that is, a pure spirit; it is the soul and body essentially united. Everything it does, including loving, must reflect its structure. If the element linked to affectivity and the heart is systematically denied or repressed, the outcome will be twofold: either one carries on wearily, out of a sense of duty and to defend one's own image, or one seeks more or less legitimate compensations, to the point of the very sad cases which we know well. At the root of many of the moral deviances of consecrated souls, the fact that there is a distorted and twisted concept of love cannot be ignored.

So we have a dual reason and urgency to rediscover love in its original unity. True and integral love is a pearl closed within two shells which are eros and agape. These two dimensions of love cannot be separated without destroying it, just as hydrogen and oxygen cannot be separated without depriving oneself of water.

## 2. The incompatibility of the two loves?

The most important reconciliation between the two dimensions of love is that practical one which happens in people's lives, but precisely for it to be made possible it is necessary to begin by reconciling eros and agape between them even theoretically, in doctrine. *Inter alia*, this will enable us to know at last what is meant by these two terms which are so often used and misunderstood.

The importance of this question arises from the fact there is a book which made the opposite thesis, the incompatibility between the two forms of love, popular throughout the Christian world. It is the book by the Swedish Lutheran theologian Anders Nygren, entitled *Agape and Eros*.[1] We can summarise his thought in these

---

[1] The Swedish original was published in Stockholm 1930; English translation, *Agape and Eros,* London, SPCK, 1982.

terms. Eros and agape describe two opposite movements: the former, the human person's ascent and climb to God, as to one's good and origin; the latter, God's descent to humanity in the incarnation and the cross of Christ: therefore, the salvation offered to humanity without merit and response on its part, which is not faith alone. The New Testament made a precise choice, using, to express love, the term agape and systematically rejecting the term eros.

Saint Paul is the one who, with the greatest purity, drew together and expressed this doctrine of love. After him, again according to Nygren's theory, such a radical antithesis was lost, almost immediately to give way to attempts at some sort of synthesis. As soon as Christianity came into cultural contact with the Greek world and the Platonic vision, already with Origen, there was a re-assessment of eros, as upward movement of the soul towards the good, as universal attraction exercised by beauty and the divine. It was along these lines that Pseudo-Dionysius the Areopagite was to write that "God is eros",[2] replacing the agape in John's famous phrase (1 Jn. 4:16) with this term.

---

2 Pseudo-Dionysius the Areopagite, *The Divine Names*, IV, 12 (pg. 3, 709ff.).

In the West a similar synthesis was carried out by Augustine with his doctrine of *caritas* understood as doctrine of the descending and gratuitous love of God for humanity (no one has spoken of "grace" in a more decisive way than him!), but also as the human person's longing for the good and for God. His is the statement: "You have made us for yourself, and our heart is restless until it rests in you";[3] his is also the image of love as a weight which attracts the soul, like the force of gravity, towards God, as the place of one's rest and pleasure.[4] For Nygren, all of this introduces an element of self-love, of one's own good, therefore of egoism, which destroys the pure gratuitousness of grace; it is a relapse into the pagan illusion of seeing salvation consisting in an ascent to God, rather than the gratuitous and unmotivated descent of God to us.

Prisoners of this impossible synthesis between eros and agape, between love of God and of self, are, for Nygren, Saint Bernard in defining the supreme degree of God's love as "loving God for himself" and a "loving oneself for

---

3  Saint Augustine, *Confessions*, I, 1.

4  *Commentary on St John's Gospel*, 26, 4-5.

God",[5] Saint Bonaventure with his ascensional *The Soul's Journey into God,* and Saint Thomas Aquinas himself who described the love of God poured out into the heart of the baptised (cf. Rom 5:5) as "the love by which he loves us and which makes us love him".[6] This, in fact, is like saying that the human person, loved by God, can in turn love God, give him something of him/herself, which destroys, still according to Nygren, the absolute gratuitousness of God's love. The same deviation happens, according to him, with Catholic mysticism. The love of the mystics, with its very strong emphasis on eros, is, for him, none other than sublimated sensual love, an attempt to establish a relationship of presumptuous reciprocity in love with God.

It was Luther who broke the ambiguity and highlighted the clear Pauline antithesis. Basing justification on faith alone, according to the Lutheran theologian, he did not exclude charity from the foundational moment of the Christian life, as Catholic theology reproaches him: rather, he liberated charity, agape, from the spurious

---

5 Cf. Saint Bernard, *De diligendo Deo,* IX, 26 – X, 27.

6 Saint Thomas Aquinas, *Commentary on the Letter to the Romans,* chap. V, Lecture 1., nn. 392-393; cf. Saint Augustine, *Homilies on the First Epistle of John,* 9, 9.

element of eros. To the formula of "faith alone", with the exclusion of works, would correspond, in Luther, the formula of "agape alone", with the exclusion of eros.

It is not my task here to ascertain whether the author correctly interpreted the thought of Luther on this matter. It must be said that Luther never set out the problem in terms of the contrast between eros and agape, as he did for faith and works. Significant, however, is the fact that Karl Barth, too, in a chapter of his *Church Dogmatics*, reaches the same conclusion as Nygren on the incompatibility between eros and agape: "Where Christian love enters, there always begins at once the unceasing controversy between itself and every other love".[7] We are completely in the realm of dialectical theology, the theology of the *aut-aut* (either-or), of the antithesis at all costs.

The repercussion of this operation is the radical worldliness and secularisation of eros. While in fact a certain theology excluded eros from agape, secular culture, for its part, was more than happy to do the opposite, excluding

---

[7] K Barth, *Church Dogmatics*, IV, 2, 727-840 [quote from pg. 736], T & T Clark, Edinburgh, 1958.

agape from eros, that is, every reference to God and to the grace of human love. Freud went to the extreme in this line of thought, reducing love to eros and eros to *libido*, to pure sexual drive. It is the stage to which love is reduced today in many manifestations of life and culture, especially in the world of entertainment, to sex appeal, the attraction of the sexes.

A few years ago I was in Madrid and the newspapers were making a great fuss about a certain art exhibition being held in the city, entitled "The tears of eros". It was an exhibition of works of art with an erotic background – pictures, drawings, sculptures – intending to highlight the inseparable link, in the experience of the modern person, between eros and *thanatos*, between love and death. The same conclusion can be reached reading Baudelaire's poetry *Les fleurs du mal* or Rimbaud's *Une Saison en Enfer*. The love which by its nature should lead to life, now leads instead to death.

### 3. Return to the synthesis

If we are unable suddenly to change the world's idea of love, we can, however, correct the theological vision which – of course without wanting to – encourages and legitimises it. This is what Benedict XVI has done in exemplary fashion in the encyclical *Deus caritas est.* He reaffirms the traditional Catholic synthesis expressing it in modern terminology:

> "Yet *eros* and *agape* – ascending love and descending love – can never be completely separated. [...] biblical faith does not set up a parallel universe, or one opposed to that primordial human phenomenon which is love, but rather accepts the whole man; it intervenes in his search for love in order to purify it and to reveal new dimensions of it" (nos. 7-8).

Eros and agape are united to the source of love which is God: "God loves", the Encyclical continues, "and his love may certainly be called *eros*, yet it is also totally *agape*" (n. 9).

Thus one understands the unusually favourable reception this papal document received in the more open and responsible secular quarters, too. It gives hope to the world. It corrects the image of a faith which touches the world at a tangent, without penetrating right into it, with the gospel image of the leaven which makes the dough ferment; to replace the idea of a kingdom of God come to "judge" the world, with that of a kingdom of God come to "save" the world, starting from the eros which is its dominating force.

I believe that the Catholic vision, which on this point coincides with the Orthodox vision, can be confirmed from an exegetical point of view, too. Those who support the idea of the incompatibility between eros and agape base their view on the fact that the New Testament carefully avoids – and, it seems, deliberately – the term eros, always using in its place agape, apart from some rare use of the term *philia*, indicating the love of friendship.

This may be true, but the conclusions drawn from it are not. It is supposed that the New Testament authors remember both the meaning that the term eros had in common usage – the so-called "vulgar" eros – and the elevated and philosophical meaning which the so-called "noble" eros had, for example, in Plato. In the popular meaning, eros indicated more or less what it means today, too, when one speaks of eroticism or erotic films, that is, the satisfaction of the sexual instinct, a debasement rather than enhancement. In the noble meaning, it indicated love for beauty, the strength which holds the world together and drives all human beings to unity, that is, that movement of ascent towards the divine which the dialectical theologians believe to be incompatible with the movement of the descent of the divine towards humanity.

It is difficult to believe that the New Testament authors, addressing simple people and of no culture, intended to warn them about the eros of Plato. They avoided the term eros for the same reason that preachers today avoid the term erotic or, if they use it, do so only in a negative sense. The reason is that, then as now, the word calls to mind love in its most selfish and sensual expression.

The meaning which the first Christians gave to the word eros is deduced clearly from the well-known text of Saint Ignatius of Antioch: "My love (eros) has been crucified, and there is no fire in me desiring to be fed...I have no delight in corruptible food, nor in the pleasures of this life".[8] Contrary to what was believed, the expression "My love (eros) has been crucified" does not mean the crucified Jesus, but the "love of myself", the attachment to earthly pleasures. As St Paul writes, "I have been crucified with Christ and I live now not with my own life" (Gal 2:19ff).

The feeling of the first Christians about eros was further compounded by the role it played in the unbridled Dionysiac cults. As soon as Christianity came into contact and dialogue

---

8 Saint Ignatius of Antioch, *Epistle to the Romans*, 7, 2.

with Greek philosophical culture, then every inhibition about eros fell away, as we have already seen. In Greek authors, the term was often used as synonymous with agape and to indicate God's love for humanity, humanity's love for God, as well as love for virtues and all things beautiful. To convince ourselves of this, a quick glance at Lampe's *A Patristic Greek Lexicon* is sufficient.[9] So the system of Nygren and Barth is therefore built on a false application of the so-called argument "of silence" *(ex silentio)*.

## 4. Christ, primary object of the human eros

The liberation of eros helps first of all human beings in love and Christian spouses, showing the beauty and dignity of the love which unites them. It helps young people to experience the allure of the other sex not as something dark, to be lived sheltered from God, but on the contrary as a gift of the Creator for their joy, if lived in the order desired by him. The Pope also alludes in his Encyclical to this positive role of eros on human love when he speaks of the path of purification of eros which leads from momentary attraction to the "forever" of matrimony" (nos. 4-5).

---

[9] Cf. G W H Lampe, *A Patristic Greek Lexicon*, Oxford 1961, pg. 550.

But the liberation of eros must help everyone, even those who are not married, the celibate, and consecrated virgins. At the start I hinted at the risk run by religious souls, which is that of a cold love, which never descends from the mind to the heart; a winter sun which gives light but no warmth. If eros means impulse, desire, attraction, we must not be afraid of feelings, much less despise and repress them. When it is love of God – wrote William of Saint-Thierry – the feeling of affection *(affectio)* is grace, too; it is not in fact nature which can instil in us such a sentiment.[10]

The Psalms are full of this yearning of the heart for God: "To you, Lord, I lift up my soul…", "My soul is thirsting for God, the living God". In *The Cloud of Unknowing*, a classic of Medieval spiritual literature, one reads: "So pay attention to this marvellous work of grace within your soul. It is always a sudden impulse and comes without warning, springing up to God like some spark from the fire…Strike that thick cloud of unknowing with the sharp dart of longing love, and on no account whatever think of giving up".[11]

---

10 William of Saint-Thierry, *Meditations*, XII, 29 (SCh 324, pg. 210).

11 *The Cloud of Unknowing*, Penguin Books Ltd., Middlesex, 1967, pgs. 57, 60.

To do that a thought, an impulse of the heart, an aspiration is sufficient. But all of that is not enough for us, and God knows that better than us. We are creatures, we live in time and in a body; we need a screen on which to project our love which is not just "the cloud of unknowing", that is the veil of obscurity behind which is hiding the God whom no one has ever seen and who lives in inaccessible light.

We know full well the response given to this question: precisely for this reason God has given us a neighbour to love! "No one has ever seen God; but as long as we love one another God will live in us and his love will be complete in us...A man who does not love the brother that he can see cannot love God, whom he has never seen" (1 Jn 4:12, 20). But we must be careful to not miss out a decisive link. Before the brother one sees there is another who can be seen and touched: the God made flesh, Jesus Christ! Between God and the neighbour there is now the Word made flesh who has re-united the two extremes in one person. And now in him is to be found the foundation of the same love of neighbour: "You did it to me".

What does all this mean for the love of God? That the primary object of our eros, of our search, desire, attraction, passion, must be the Christ

> "Human love is pre-ordained to the Saviour from the beginning, as its model and end, almost like a casket so large and wide as to be able to receive God [...]. The desire of the soul goes only to Christ. Here is the place of its rest, since he alone is the good, the truth and everything which inspires love".[12]

Resounding clearly throughout the whole of Western monastic spirituality is Saint Benedict's maxim: "Prefer nothing whatsoever to the love of Christ". This does not mean limiting the horizon of Christian love from God to Christ; it means loving God in the manner in which he wants to be loved. "The Father himself loves you for loving me" (Jn 16:27). This is not a mediated love, almost by proxy, by which whoever loves Jesus "it is as if" they love the Father. No, Jesus is an immediate mediator; loving him then *ipso facto* one loves the Father, too. "To see me is to see the Father", who loves me loves the Father.

It is true that one does not even see Christ, but he is there; he is risen, he lives, he is beside us, more truly than the most enamoured bridegroom is beside the bride. And this is the crucial point: to think of Christ not as a person from the past,

---

12  N Cabasilas, *Vita in Cristo*, II, 9 (pgs. 150, 560-561).

but as the risen and living Lord, with whom I can speak, whom I can also kiss if I want, sure that my kiss ends not on paper or the wood of a crucifix, but on a face and the lips of living flesh (even if spiritualised), happy to receive my kiss.

The beauty and fullness of the consecrated life depend on the quality of our love for Christ. It alone is capable of protecting against the deviations of the heart. Jesus is the perfect man; at an infinitely superior level are found in him all those qualities and concerns which a man seeks in a woman and a woman in a man. His love does not necessarily subtract us from the allure of creatures and in particular the attraction of the other sex (this is part of our nature which God himself has created and does not want to destroy); however, it gives us the strength to overcome these attractions with a stronger attraction. "Chaste", writes Saint John Climacus, "is the one who drives out eros with Eros".[13]

Does all of this perhaps destroy the gratuitousness of agape, pretending to give to God something in exchange for his love? Does it cancel grace, as Nygren believes? Not at all.

---

[13] Saint John Climacus, *Stairway to Paradise*, XV, 98 (pgs. 88, 880).

In fact it exalts it. What in fact, in this way, can we give God if not what we have received from him? "We are to love, then, because he loved us first" (1 Jn 4:19). The love we give to Christ is his own love for us which we give back to him, just as in an echo of a voice.

Where then is the novelty and beauty of this love which we call eros? The echo gives back to God his own love, but enriched, coloured or perfumed by our freedom. And that is all he wants. Our freedom repays it completely. Not just that, but a thing unheard of, writes Cabasilas, "receiving from us the gift of love in exchange for all that he has given us, he holds himself our debtor".[14] The idea which opposes eros and agape is based on another well-known antithesis, that between grace and freedom, and even on the very denial of freedom in the fallen humanity.

I have tried to imagine, Venerable Fathers and brothers, what the risen Jesus would say if, as he did in his earthly life when he entered into the synagogue on the Sabbath, he now came and sat in my place and explained to us in person the love he desires from us. I want to

---

14 N Cabasilas, *Vita in Cristo*, VI, 4.

share with you, in simplicity, what I think he would say to us; it will serve as our examination of conscience on love:

Passionate love:
Is putting me always in the first place.
Is seeking to please me at every moment.
Is comparing your desires with my desire.
Is living before me as friend, confidant,
 bridegroom, and being happy with it.
Is being worried if you think you are
 far from me.
Is being full of happiness when I am with you.
Is being ready to make great sacrifices
 in order not to lose me.
Is preferring to live poor and unknown with
 me, rather than rich and famous without me.
Is speaking to me as the dearest friend
 at every moment.
Is trusting in me looking to the future.
Is desiring to lose yourself in me as the goal
 of your existence.

If it seems to you, as it seems to me, that you are still a long way off from this goal, let us not be discouraged. We have someone who can help us to reach it if we ask him. Let us pray with faith, *Veni, Sancte Spiritus, reple tuorum corda fidelium et tui amoris in eis ignem accende:*

Come, Holy Spirit, fill the hearts of your faithful and enkindle in them the fire of your love.

# II

# GOD ALSO DESIRES MAN

THE FIRST and fundamental proclamation which the Church is charged to bring to the world and which the world expects from the Church is that of God's love. But in order for the evangelisers to be able to transmit this certainty, they themselves must be intimately permeated with it, it must be the light of their lives. At least in part this is the aim of this present meditation.

The expression "love of God" has two very different meanings: one in which God is the object and the other in which God is subject; one which indicates our love for God and the other indicating God's love for us. The human person, more inclined by nature to be active rather than passive, more to feel a creditor than debtor, has always given precedence to the first meaning, to what we do for God. Christian preaching, too, has followed this path, speaking, in certain eras, almost solely of the "duty" to love God *(De diligendo Deo)*.

But biblical revelation gives precedence to the second meaning: to the love "of" God, not love "for" God. Aristotle said that God moves the world "because he is *loved*", that is because he is object of love and final cause of all creatures.[15] But the Bible says exactly the opposite, that God creates and moves the world because he *loves* the world. The most important thing about God's love therefore is not that the human person loves God, but that God loves the human person and loves that person "first": "This is the love I mean: not our love for God, but God's love for us" (1 Jn 4:10). Everything else depends on this, including our own ability to love God: "We are to love, then, because he loved us first" (1 Jn 4:19).

## 1. The love of God in eternity

John is the man of great leaps. In piecing together the earthly history of Christ, the others stopped at his birth from Mary, but he makes the great leap backwards, from time to eternity: "In the beginning was the Word". He does the same with love. All the others, including Paul, spoke about

---

15 Aristotle, *Metaphysics*, XII, 7, 1072b.

the love of God manifesting itself in history and culminating in Christ's death; John goes back beyond history. He does not present us with just a God who *loves*, but a God who *is* love: "In the beginning was love, love was with God and love was God": hence we can unravel his statement: "God is love" (1 Jn 4:16).

About this, Saint Augustine wrote: "If nothing were said in praise of love throughout the pages of this epistle, if nothing whatever throughout the other pages of the Scriptures, and this one thing only were all we were told by the voice of the Spirit of God, 'For Love is God'; nothing more ought we to require".[16] The whole of the Bible simply "narrates the love of God".[17] This is the news which sustains and explains everything else. The existence of God can be discussed endlessly, and not just from today; but I believe that the most important thing is not to know whether God exists or not, but if he is love.[18] Let's assume he existed but was not love, there would be more to fear than rejoice at his existence, as in fact has happened among

---

16 Saint Augustine, *Homilies on the First Epistle of John*, 7, 4.

17 Saint Augustine, *De catechizandis rudibus*, I, 8, 4 (PL 40, 319).

18 Cf. S Kierkegaard, *Edifying Discourses in a Different Vein*, 3; *Gospel of Sufferings*, IV.

various peoples and civilisations. Christian faith assures us of precisely this: God exists and is love!

The starting point for our journey, therefore, is the Trinity. Why do Christians believe in the Trinity? The answer is: because they believe God is love. Where God is perceived as supreme Law or supreme Power there is obviously no need for a plurality of persons and so the Trinity is not understood. Law and power can be exercised by only one person, love, no.

There is no love which is not of something or someone, just as – as the philosopher Husserl says – there is no knowledge which is not knowledge of something. Who does God love to be defined as love? Humanity? But people have existed only for thousands of years; before then, who did God love to be defined as love? He cannot have begun to be love at a certain point in time, because God cannot change his essence. The cosmos? But the universe has existed for billions of years; before, who did God love to be able to define himself as love? Himself? But to love oneself is not love, it is selfishness or, as the psychologists say, narcissism.

And here is the answer of Christian revelation which the Church received from Christ and explained in its credo. God is love in himself, before time, because he has always had in himself a Son, the Word, whom he loves with an infinite love which is the Holy Spirit. In each love there are always three realities or subjects: one who loves, one who is loved and the love which unites them.

## 2. The love of God in creation

When this love at the source extends in time, we have the history of salvation. The first stage of this is *creation*. By its nature, love is *diffusivum sui*, that is it inclines towards communicating itself. Since "action follows being", being love, God creates through love. "Why did God make us?": thus asked the second question of the catechism, and the response: "To know him, love him and serve him in this life and to be happy with him for ever in the next". A correct answer, but incomplete. It replies to the answer about the final cause: "for what aim, to what end has God created us"; it does not respond to the question about the causal cause: "why did he create us, what drove him to create us". To this question one must not respond: "so that we might love him", but "because he loved us".

On this point how far the Christian vision of the origin of the universe is from that of atheist scientism! One of the most profound sufferings for a young boy or girl is to discover one day that they are in the world by chance, not wanted, not expected, even perhaps through a parental mistake. A certain atheist scientism seems committed to inflicting this type of suffering on the whole of humanity. No one would be able to convince us of the fact that we had been created out of love better than Saint Catherine of Siena does in her passionate prayer to the Trinity:

> "How, then, did you create, O Eternal Father, this your creature? [...] Fire constrained you. O ineffable love, even though in your light you saw all the iniquities, which your creature would commit against your infinite goodness, you looked as if you did not see, but rested your sight on the beauty of your creature, whom you, as mad and drunk with love, fell in love with and out of love you drew her to yourself giving her being in your image and likeness. You, eternal truth, have declared to me your truth, that is, that love constrained you to create her."

This is not just agape, love of mercy, of giving, and of descent; it is also eros and in its pure state; it is attraction towards the object of love itself, admiration and allurement with its beauty.

## 3. The love of God in revelation

The second stage in the history of the love of God is *revelation*, Scripture. God speaks to us of his love above all in the prophets. It says in Hosea:

> "When Israel was a child I loved him [...]. I myself taught Ephraim to walk, I took them in my arms [...]. I led them with reins of kindness, with leading-strings of love. I was like someone who lifts an infant close against his cheek; stooping down to him I gave him his food [...]. Ephraim, how could I part with you? [...] My heart recoils from it, my whole being trembles at the thought" (Hos 11:1-4).

We find the same language in Isaiah: "Does a woman forget her baby at the breast, or fail to cherish the son of her womb?" (Is 49:15) and Jeremiah: "Is Ephraim, then, so dear a son to me, a child so favoured, that after each threat of mine I must still remember him, still be deeply moved for him, and let my tenderness yearn over him?" (Jer 31:20). In these oracles, the love of God is expressed at the same time as paternal and maternal love: a concerned love, a driven love, a correcting love, like that of every father; a "visceral" love, of tenderness, of acceptance and compassion, like that of every mother.

The human person knows by experience another type of love, that of which it is said "is strong as Death...the flash of it as a flash of fire" (cf. Song 8:6), and God has also had recourse to this type of love, in the Bible, to give us an idea of his passionate love for us. All the phases and events of spousal love are evoked and used for this end: the enchantment of love as it arises at the betrothal (cf. Jer 2:2); the fullness of joy on the day of matrimony (cf. Is 62:5); the tragedy of the break-up (cf. Hos 2:4ff.) and finally the rebirth, full of hope, of the ancient bond (cf. Hos 2:16; Is 54:8).

*Spousal love* is, fundamentally, a love of desire and choice. If it is true, therefore, that the human person desires God, the opposite, mysteriously, is also true, that is, that God desires the human person, wants and respects his/her love, rejoices in it "as the bridegroom rejoices in his bride" (Is 62:5)! As the Pope points out in *Deus caritas est*, the nuptial metaphor which runs throughout almost the whole of the Bible and inspires the language of "covenant" is the best confirmation that God's love for us is also eros and agape, it is giving and seeking at the same time. It cannot be reduced just to mercy, to a "being charitable" to humanity, in the most reductive sense of the word.

## 4. The love of God in the incarnation

So we come to the culminating stage of the love of God, the *incarnation*: "God loved the world so much that he gave his only Son" (Jn 3:16). In the face of the incarnation we ask ourselves the same question as for creation. Why did God make himself man? *Cur Deus homo?* For a long time the answer was: to redeem us from sin. Duns Scotus went into this answer, making love the fundamental reason for the incarnation, just like all the other *ad extra* works of the Trinity.

God, said Scotus, first of all loves himself; secondly, he wants there to be other beings to love him *(secundo vult alios habere condiligentes)*. If he decides the incarnation of his Son it is because he wants another being to exist who loves him with the greatest love possible outside himself.[19] So the incarnation would have taken place even if Adam had not sinned. Christ is the first thought and the first desire, the "first-born of all creation" (Col 1:15), not the solution to a problem which came about following Adam's sin.

But Scotus' answer, too, is incomplete and must be completed according to what Scripture

---

19 Duns Scotus, *Opus Oxoniense,* I, d. 17, q. 3, n. 31; Rep., II, d. 27, q. un., n. 3.

tells us about the love of God. God wanted the Son's incarnation not just to have someone outside himself *to love him* in a manner worthy of himself, but also and above all to have outside himself someone *to love* in a manner worthy of himself! And this is the Son made man, in whom the Father "is well-pleased" and with whom we are all made "children in the Son".

Christ is the supreme proof of God's love for humanity not just in the objective sense, in the manner of an inanimate pledge given to someone of one's own love; it is also so in the subjective sense. In other words, it is not just the proof of the love of God, but it is also the love itself of God which has assumed a human form in order to be able to love and be loved from within our situation. In the beginning was love and "love was made flesh": so a very ancient Christian writing paraphrases the words of the Prologue of John.[20]

Saint Paul coins a special expression for this new modality of God's love, calling it "the love of God made visible in Christ Jesus our Lord" (Rom 8:39). If, as was said in the preceding chapter, all our love for God must be expressed

---

20 *Evangelium veritatis* (from the Nag-Hammadi codices)

concretely in love for Christ, it is because all God's love for us is, first of all, expressed and gathered in Christ.

## 5. If this is not love...

The revulsion of many exegetes and theologians in accepting the "expiatory" character of Christ's death, even accepting the very death of Jesus as desired by the Father and freely accepted by the Son,[21] depends, I believe, on the fact that, in the study of Scripture, one starts from every possible and imaginable "pre-understanding" *(Vorverständnis)* apart from the unique one offered to us: God is love and all he does – including the death of his Son – is love.

"God did not spare his own Son, but gave him up to benefit us all" (Rom 8:32): as in the story of the sacrifice of Isaac from which it is taken (Gen 22:16), this phrase does not mean: "God did not spare from justice even his Son"; it means "God did not spare his own Son, but made the great sacrifice to give him up for all of us". If this is not love...

---

21 Cf. J Ratzinger – Benedict XVI, *Jesus of Nazareth, Part II*, Ignatius Press, San Francisco, 2011.

The history of God's love does not end, however, with Easter; it carries on to Pentecost which makes present and operative "the love of God made visible in Christ Jesus" up to the end of the world. "Remain in my love" (Jn 15:9), said Jesus, and John adds: "We can know that we are living in him and he is living in us because he lets us share his Spirit" (1 Jn 4:13). We are not forced to live only on the memory of God's love, as something of the past. "The love of God has been poured into our hearts by the Holy Spirit which has been given us" (Rom 5:5).

What is this love which has been poured into our hearts in baptism? Is it God's feeling for us? His benevolent disposition to us? An inclination? That is, something *intentional*? It is much more; it is something *real*. It is, literally, the love *of* God, that is, the love which flows in the Trinity between Father and Son and which in the incarnation has assumed a human form and now is participated in by us in the form of "in-dwelling". "My Father will love him and we shall come to him and make our home with him" (Jn 14:23).

We become "sharers in the divine nature" (2 Pet 1:4), that is sharers in the divine love. St John of the Cross explains that we come to find ourselves by grace within the vortex of love which flows, from all time, between the Father and the Son;[22] or better still: between the vortex of love which now passes, in heaven, between the Father and his Son Jesus Christ, risen from the dead, of whom we are the members.

## 6. We have believed in the love of God!

What I have poorly traced is the objective revelation of the love of God in history. What shall we do, what will we say after having heard how much God loves us? A first answer is: to love God in return! Isn't this perhaps the first and greatest commandment of the law? Yes, but that comes afterwards. Another possible answer: to love each other as God has loved us! Isn't it perhaps John the evangelist who says, if God has loved us, "we too should love one another" (1 Jn 4:11)? Yes, but this, too, comes afterwards. First there is something else to be done: to believe in the love of God! After having said that "God is love", John the evangelist exclaims: "We ourselves have known and put our faith in God's love towards ourselves" (1 Jn 4:16).

Faith, therefore. But here it is a special faith: faith-wonder, incredulous faith (a paradox, I

---

22 Cf. Saint John of the Cross, *A Spiritual Canticle,* v. 38.

know, but true!), the faith which is unable to understand what it believes, even if it believes it. How is it possible that God, extremely happy in his calm eternity, had the desire not just to create us, but also to come in person to suffer in the midst of us? How is this possible? Here, this is the faith-wonder, the faith which makes us happy.

The great convert and apologist for the faith Clive Staples Lewis (the author, by the way, of the Narnia narrative cycle, recently brought to the big screen) wrote an unusual novel entitled *The Screwtape Letters*. They are the letters of an old devil writing to a young and inexperienced devil on the earth trying to seduce a young Londoner who has just returned to the practice of the Christian faith. The aim is to instruct him on the way to achieve his goal. It is a modern, magnificent treatise of morals and ascetics, to be read from back-to-front, that is, doing exactly the opposite of what is suggested.

At a certain point the author has us observe a kind of discussion which takes place between the demons. They cannot understand how "the Enemy" (as they call God) can really love "human vermin and really desire their freedom". They are certain it cannot be so. It must of course be deceit, a trick. We are making inquiries about that, they say, from the day on which "Our

Father" (so they call Lucifer), precisely for just this reason, distanced himself from him; we still haven't discovered it, but one day we will.[23] God's love for his creatures is, for them, the mystery of mysteries. And I think that, at least in this, the demons are right.

It would seem to be a facile and enjoyable faith; instead it is perhaps the most difficult thing for us human creatures. Do we really believe that God loves us? No, we don't really believe that ourselves, or at least we don't really believe enough! Because if we really believed, immediately our lives, ourselves, things, events, pain itself, all would be changed before our very eyes. This very day we would be with him in paradise, because paradise is simply this: to enjoy the love of God in fullness.

The world has made it increasingly difficult to believe in love. Whoever has been betrayed or wounded once is afraid to love or be loved, because that person knows how much it can hurt to discover oneself betrayed again. So, the ranks of those who are unable to believe in the love of God increases more and more; indeed, to believe in any love. Disenchantment and cynicism the hallmarks of our secularised

---

23 C S Lewis, *The Screwtape Letters*, 1942, chap. XIX.

culture. On a personal level, then, there is the experience of our poverty and misery which makes us say: "Yes, this love of God is beautiful, but it is not for me! I am not worthy...".

Humanity needs to know that God loves humanity and no one is better suited than the disciples of Christ to bring them this good news. Others, in the world, share with Christians the fear of God, concern for social justice and respect for the person, the commitment to peace and tolerance; but no-one – I repeat no-one – except the Bible says to the human person that they are loved by God, first, and with merciful love and love of desire: with eros and agape.

Saint Paul suggests to us a method for applying the light of the love of God to our concrete existence. He writes: "Nothing therefore can come between us and the love of Christ, even if we are troubled or worried, or being persecuted, or lacking food or clothes, or being threatened or even attacked. [...] These are the trials through which we triumph, by the power of him who loved us" (Rom 8:35-37). The dangers and enemies of the love of God which he lists are those which he has, in fact, experienced in his life: anguish, persecution, the sword... (cf. 2 Cor 11:23ff.). He reviews them in his mind and states that none of them is so strong as to compare with the thought of the love of God.

We are invited to do the same as him: to examine our life, just as it presents itself, to bring to the surface the fears lurking there, the sadness, the threats, the problems, that physical or moral defect, that painful memory which humiliates us, and to expose everything to the light of the thought that God loves me.

From his own personal life, the Apostle extends his outlook over the world that surrounds him: "For I am certain of this: neither death nor life, no angel, no prince, nothing that exists, nothing still to come, not any power, or height or depth, nor any created thing, can ever come between us and the love of God made visible in Christ Jesus our Lord" (Rom 8:37-39). He observes "his" world, with the powers that then made it threatening: death with its mystery, the present life with its illusions, the heavenly or infernal powers which induced so much fear into ancient man.

We can do the same: look at the world which surrounds and frightens us. The "height" and the "depth" are for us now the infinitely great on high and the infinitely low, the universe and the atom. Everything is ready to crush us; the human person is weak and alone, in a universe much greater than him or her and which in addition has become more threatening, in the wake of the scientific discoveries which humanity has brought about and is unable to dominate, as revealed dramatically by the events of the nuclear reactors in Fukushima.

Everything can be questioned, all the certainties can fail us, but never this: that God loves us and is stronger than everything. There is a psalm which seems to have been written after a cataclysm like that which recently struck Japan – earthquake, tsunami and flood – because, in the certainty that God is with them, people find the strength to get up again after every adversity:

"God is our shelter, our strength,
ever ready to help in time of trouble,
so we shall not be afraid when the earth gives way,
when mountains tumble into the sea,
and its waters roar and seethe,
the mountains tottering as it heaves"
(Ps 46:1-3).

# III

# LET CHARITY BE WITHOUT PRETENCE

### 1. Love your neighbour as yourself

A CURIOUS thing has been noticed. In its course, the river Jordan forms two seas: the Sea of Galilee and the Dead Sea, but while the Sea of Galilee is a sea teeming with life and is among the most abundant fishing waters on earth, the Dead Sea is precisely that, a "dead" sea, there is no trace of life in it or around it, just saltiness. And yet it is the same waters of the Jordan. The explanation, at least in part, lies in this: the Sea of Galilee receives the waters of the Jordan but doesn't keep them to itself, it drains them in such a way that they can irrigate the whole Jordan valley. The Dead Sea receives the waters of the Jordan and keeps them for itself, it has no outlets, not a drop of water seeps out of it. It is a symbol. We cannot limit ourselves to receiving love, we must also give it. This is what we want to reflect on in this meditation. The water that Jesus gives us must become "a spring inside..." (Jn 4:14).

Having reflected in the first two meditations on the love of God as *gift*, the time has come to meditate also on the duty of loving, and in particular on the *duty* of loving one's neighbour. The link between the two loves is expressed in a keynote manner by the word of God: "My dear people, since God has loved us so much, we too should love one another" (1 Jn 4:11).

"You must love your neighbour as yourself" was one of the ancient commandments, written in the Law of Moses (Lev 19:18) and Jesus himself quotes it as such (Lk 10:27). How come then Jesus calls it "his" commandment and the "new" commandment? The answer is that with him the object, subject and motive of the love of neighbour have changed.

First of all the *object* has changed, that is the neighbour to love. That person is no longer just the fellow countryman or at the most the guest living with the people, but everyone, even the stranger (the Samaritan!), even the enemy. It is true that the second part of the phrase "You must love your neighbour and hate your enemy" (Mt 5:43) is not found word-for-word in the Old Testament, but it assumes the general direction of it, expressed in the law of retaliation "eye for eye, tooth for tooth" (Lev 24:20), especially when compared with Jesus' demands of his followers:

> "But I say this to you: love your enemies and pray for those who persecute you; in this way you will be sons of your Father in heaven, for he causes his sun to rise on bad men as well as good, and his rain to fall on honest and dishonest men alike. For if you love those who love you, what right have you to claim any credit? Even the tax collectors do as much, do they not? And if you save your greetings for your brothers, are you doing anything exceptional? Even the pagans do as much, do they not? (Mt 5:44-47).

The *subject* of love of neighbour has changed, too, that is, the meaning of the word neighbour. It is not the other; it is me; it is not the one who is close, but the one who *comes* close. In the parable of the Good Samaritan Jesus demonstrates that there is no need to wait passively for the neighbour to appear on our street, with flashing lights and sirens sounding. The neighbour is you, that is, what you can become. The neighbour is not ready-made, one has a neighbour only if one becomes neighbour to someone.

Above all, the *criterion* or measure of love of neighbour has changed. Up until Jesus the model was self-love: "as yourself". It was said that God could not have chosen a more secure "peg" than this on which to hang the love of neighbour; he would not have achieved the same aim even if he had said: "You must love your neighbour as you love your God!", because on the love of God – that is, on what it is to love God – the human person can still cheat, but on love of self, no. The human person knows full well what it means, in every circumstance, to love oneself; it is a mirror which is always before us, with no escape.[24]

But instead there is an escape, and so therefore Jesus replaces it with another model and another measure: "This is my commandment: love one another, *as I have loved you*" (Jn 15:12). The human person can love him/herself in a mistaken way, that is, to desire evil, not good, to love vice, not virtue. If such a person loves others "as him/herself" and wants for others what they want for themselves, how unfortunate is the person loved in this way! On the other hand, we know where the love of Jesus leads us: to truth, to good, to the

---

24 Cf. S Kierkegaard, *Gli atti dell'amore*, Milan, 1983, pg. 163 (English translation: *Works of Love*, London, Collins, 1962)

Father. Whoever follows him "does not walk in the darkness". He has loved us, giving his life for us when we were sinners, that is, enemies (Rom 5:6ff.).

So one can understand what the evangelist John means by his seemingly contradictory statement: "My dear people, this is not a new commandment that I am writing to tell you, but an old commandment that you were given from the beginning, the original commandment which was the message brought to you. Yet in another way, what I am writing to you is a new commandment" (1 Jn 2:7-8). The commandment of love of neighbour is "old" literally, but "new" in the very newness of the gospel. New, explains Pope Benedict XVI in the second volume of his book on Jesus Christ, because it is no longer just "law", but also, and even before, "grace". It is based on communion with Christ, made possible by the gift of the Spirit.[25]

With Jesus one passes from the two-fold relationship: "What the other does to you, you do to him", to the three-fold relationship: "What God has done to you, you do it to another", or, starting from the other direction: "What you have done to the other, is what God will do with

---

25 J Ratzinger - Benedict XVI, op. cit.

you". There are innumerable phrases of Jesus and the apostles which repeat this idea: "Just as God has forgiven you, so you must forgive each other"; "If in your heart you do not forgive your enemies, nor will your Father forgive you". Rooted out is the excuse: "But he doesn't love me, he offends me...". This is to do with him, not you. What must interest you is simply what you do to others and how you behave in the face of what others do to you.

There remains, however, the response to the main question: why this unique change in direction from love of God to love of neighbour? Wouldn't it be more logical to expect: "As I have loved you, so you must love me", rather than: "As I have loved you, so you must love each other"? Here lies the difference between love purely eros and the love of eros and agape together. Purely erotic love is a closed circuit: "Love me, Alfredo, love me just as much as I love you": so sings Violetta in Verdi's *La Traviata:* I love you, you love me. The love of agape is an open circuit: it comes from God and returns to him, but goes through one's neighbour. Jesus himself inaugurated this new type of love: "As the Father has loved me, so I have loved you" (Jn 15:9).

Saint Catherine of Siena has provided the simplest and most convincing explanation of the reason for this. She has God say:

"I ask you to love me with the same love with which I love you. But for me you cannot do this, for I loved you without being loved. Whatever love you have for me you owe me, so you love me not gratuitously but out of duty, while I love you not out of duty but gratuitously. So you cannot give me the kind of love I ask of you. This is why I have put you among your neighbours: so that you can do for them what you cannot do for me – that is, love them without any concern for thanks and without looking for any profit for yourself. And whatever you do for them I will consider done for me".[26]

## 2. Love each other with a sincere heart

After these general reflections on the commandment of love of neighbour, it is time to speak about the qualities with which this new love must be clothed. There are basically two: it must be a sincere love and an effective love, a love of the heart and a love, so to speak, of the hands. This time we will focus on the first quality and will do so by allowing ourselves to be guided by the great poet of love, Saint Paul.

---

26 Saint Catherine of Siena, *Dialogue*, 64.

The second part of the Letter to the Romans is a whole series of recommendations about mutual love within the Christian community: "Do not let your love be a pretence [...]; love each other as much as brothers should, and have a profound respect for each other..." (Rom 12:9ff.). "Avoid getting into debt, except the debt of mutual love. If you love your fellow men you have carried out your obligations" (Rom 13:8).

To grasp the soul which unites all these recommendations, the basic idea, or, better still, the "feeling" which Paul has about charity, it is necessary to start from the initial phrase: "Do not let your love be a pretence!" This is not one of many exhortations, but the background from which all others derive. It contains the secret of charity. With the help of the Holy Spirit, let us try to grasp such a secret.

The original term used by Paul and which is translated as "without pretence" is *anhypòkritos*, that is, without hypocrisy. This word is a kind of pilot-light; it is, in fact, a rare term which is used, in the New Testament, almost exclusively to define Christian love. The expression "sincere love" *(anhypòkritos)* returns again in 2 Corinthians 6:6 and in 1 Peter 1:22. This latter text enables us to grasp, with total certainty, the meaning of the term in question, because it is explained with a round-about expression;

sincere love, it says, consists in loving in sincerity "and from the heart".

Saint Paul, therefore, with that simple statement: "Do not let your love be a pretence!" brings the discourse to the very root of charity, to the heart. What is asked of love is that it be true, authentic, not false. Just as wine, in order to be "sincere", must be pressed from the grape, so love must be from the heart. Here, too, the Apostle faithfully echoes the thought of Jesus; he, in fact, had indicated, repeatedly and with force, the heart as the "place" where the value of what the human person does is decided, what is pure, or impure, in a person's life (cf. Mt 15:19).

We can speak of a Pauline intuition about charity; it consists in revealing, behind the visible and external universe of charity, made up of deeds and words, another entirely internal universe, which is, compared to the first, what the soul is for the body. We find this intuition again in the other great text on charity, 1 Corinthians 13. On close examination, what Saint Paul says there concerns entirely this internal charity, the dispositions and sentiments of charity: charity is patient, it is kind, it is not jealous, it is never angry, it is always ready to excuse, to trust, to hope...There is nothing here, *per se* and directly, about *doing* good, or the works of charity, but everything harks back to the root of *wanting* what is good.

It is the Apostle himself who clarifies the difference between the two spheres of charity, saying that the greatest act of external charity – distributing to the poor all one's own possessions – would all be of no benefit, without internal charity (cf. 1 Cor 13:3). It would be the opposite of "sincere" charity. Hypocritical charity, in fact, is precisely that which externally manifests something which has no correspondence in the heart. In this case, there is an appearance of charity, which can, at worst, hide selfishness, self-pursuit, manipulation of one's brother, or even simply a prick of conscience.

It would be a fatal error to contrast charity of the heart and charity of deed, or take refuge in internal charity, to find therein a type of alibi for the lack of effective charity. Furthermore, to say that, without charity, "I gain nothing" even in giving everything to the poor, does not mean that there is no point in doing that and it is useless; rather it means that "I" gain nothing, while it may be of benefit to the poor recipient. It is not, therefore, lessening the importance of the works of charity (we will see this more clearly in the next chapter), but ensuring they have a secure foundation against selfishness and its infinite cunning. Saint Paul wants

Christians to be "planted in love and built on love" (Eph 3:17), that is, that love may be the root and foundation of everything.

To love sincerely means to love at this depth, where you can no longer lie, because you are alone in front of yourself, alone in front of the mirror of your conscience, under God's gaze. "It remains", writes Augustine, "that that man loves his brother, who before God, where God alone sees, assures his own heart, and questions his heart whether he does this indeed for love of the brethren; and his witness is that eye which penetrates the heart, where man cannot look".[27] Paul's love for the Jews was sincere love, therefore, if he was able to say: "What I want to say now is no pretence; I say it in union with Christ – it is the truth – my conscience in union with the Holy Spirit assures me of it too. What I want to say is this: my sorrow is so great, my mental anguish so endless, I would willingly be condemned and be cut off from Christ if it could help my brothers of Israel, my own flesh and blood" (Rom 9:1-3). Showing there are only two witnesses, his own conscience and the Holy Spirit, to which one cannot lie.

---

27 Saint Augustine, *Homily on the First Epistle of John*, 6, 2 (PL 35, 2020).

To be genuine, therefore, Christian charity must start from within, from the heart; the works of mercy from "*sincere* compassion" (Col 3:12). However, we must immediately state that here it is something much more radical than simple "internalisation", that is, a shifting of the emphasis from the external practice of charity to the internal practice. This is only the first step. Internalisation leads to divinisation! The Christian, said Saint Peter, is the one who loves "with a true heart": but what heart? With the "new heart and new Spirit" received in baptism!

When a Christian loves in this way, it is God loving through that person; he or she becomes a channel of God's love. Something similar happens with consolation, which is none other but a quality of loving: "[Blessed be the Father] the God of all consolation, who comforts us in all our sorrows, so that we can offer others, in their sorrows, the consolation that we have received from God ourselves" (2 Cor 1:4). We console with the consolation with which we are consoled by God, we love with the love with which we are loved by God. Not with something different. This explains the seemingly disproportionate reverberation which a very simple act of love sometimes has, often even hidden, the hope and light which it creates within.

## 3. Love edifies

When love is spoken about in the apostolic writings, it is never in the abstract, in general terms. The background is always the building up of the Christian community. In other words, the first area for the exercise of charity must be the Church and more concretely still the community in which one lives, the people with whom one has daily contact. This must happen today, too, in particular at the heart of the Church, between those who work in close contact with the Supreme Pontiff.

For a certain time, in antiquity, the term love, agape, was used not just for the fraternal meal which Christians took together, but also for the whole Church.[28] The martyr Saint Ignatius of Antioch greets the Church of Rome as that "which presides over love (agape)", that is over "Christian fraternity", over all the Churches.[29] This phrase affirms not just the *fact* of the primacy of Rome, but also its *nature*, or the way of exercising it: that is, in love. The phrase can be translated in two ways: the Roman Church

---

28 G W H Lampe, op. cit., pg. 8.

29 Saint Ignatius of Antioch, *The Epistle to the Romans*, opening greeting.

"presides over charity", or "presides *in* charity", with charity.

The Church has urgent need of an outburst of charity to heal its wounds. In one of his addresses Paul VI said: "The Church needs to feel flowing again through all its human faculties the wave of love, that love which is called charity, and which is precisely poured into our hearts by the Holy Spirit which has been given to us".[30] Only love heals. It is the oil of the Samaritan. Oil also because it must float above everything as oil does above water. "Over all these clothes, to keep them together and to complete them, put on love" (Col 3:14). Above everything, *super omnia!* Therefore over discipline and authority, too, even if, obviously, the same discipline and authority can be expressions of charity.

An important area on which to work is that of mutual judgement. Paul wrote to the Romans: "This is also why you should never pass judgement on a brother or treat him with contempt [...] far from passing judgement on each other..." (Rom 14:10, 13). Before him Jesus had

---

30 Discourse at the General Audience of 29 November 1972 (*Insegnamenti di Paolo VI*, Vatican Polyglot Press, X, pgs. 1210f.).

said: "Do not judge, and you will not be judged. [...] Why do you observe the splinter in your brother's eye and never notice the plank in your own?" (Mt 7:1-3). He calls a splinter the sin of the neighbour (the sin judged), whatever it may be, compared to the sin of the one judging (the sin of judgement), which is a plank.

The discourse on judgements is certainly sensitive and complex and cannot be left mid-sentence, without making it suddenly seem hardly realistic. How is it possible, in fact, to live without judging at all? Judgement is implicit in us even in a glance. We cannot observe, listen, live, without making assessments, that is, without judging. A parent, a superior, a confessor, a judge, whoever has a responsibility over others, must judge. Sometimes, in fact, judgement is exactly the type of service which one is called to render to society or to the Church.

In fact, it is not so much the judgement which must be cut out from our hearts, but rather the poison of our judgement! That is, malice, condemnation. In Luke's version, Jesus' commandment "Do not judge, and you will not be judged yourselves" is followed immediately, as if to explain the meaning of these words, by the command: "Do not condemn, and you will not be condemned yourselves" (Lk 6:37). *Per se,* judgement is a neutral action, judgement can end either in condemnation or absolution and justification. It is negative judgements which are taken up and banned by the word of God, those which along with sin condemn the sinner, too, those which aim more at punishment than correction of the brother.

Another qualifying point about sincere charity is respect: "Have a profound respect for each other" (Rom 12:10). To respect one's brother there is a need for not too much self-esteem, or self-assurance; there is a need, says the Apostle, "not to exaggerate [one's] real importance" (Rom 12:3). People with too high an idea of themselves are like someone who, at night, has a source of intense light before their eyes: that person is unable to see anything beyond it; is unable to see the lights of their brothers and sisters, their merits and their values.

"Minimising" must become a preferred verb in relations with others: to minimise our merits and the defects of others; not the contrary which is to minimise our defects and the merits of others, as, instead, we are often led to do. There is a fable of Aesop about this which, in the re-working of it by La Fontaine, says this:

"As in this world we're but way-farers,
Kind Heaven has made us wallet-bearers.
The pouch behind our own defects must store.
The faults of others lodge in that before".[31]

We must simply turn things upside down: put our defects in the bag we have in front and the defects of others in the one behind. Saint James warns: "Brothers, do not slander one another" (Jas 4:11). Tittle-tattle has today changed its name, it is called *gossip*. It seems to have become something innocent, indeed it is one of the things which most poisons our living side-by-side. It is not sufficient not to slander others; there is a need also to stop others doing it in our presence, to make them understand, perhaps by silence, that you don't agree. What a different atmosphere there is where James' warning is taken seriously! At one time in many public places there would be a sign: "No smoking", or "No swearing". It wouldn't be bad to replace them in some places with "No gossiping!"

We conclude with a type of examination of conscience on our love for others, based on Paul's hymn to charity in his First Letter to the Corinthians (13:4-7). It will suffice to re-read it

---

31 J de la Fontaine, *Fables*, I, 7.

slowly, and following every statement with a question: Love is patient: am I patient?

"Love is always patient and kind;
it is never jealous;
love is never boastful or conceited;
it is never rude or selfish;
it does not take offence, and is not resentful.
Love takes no pleasure in other people's sins
but delights in the truth;
it is always ready to excuse, to trust, to hope,
and to endure whatever comes."

# IV

# AN EFFECTIVE LOVE: THE SOCIAL SIGNIFICANCE OF THE GOSPEL

### 1. The exercise of charity

IN THE previous meditation we learned from Paul that Christian love must be sincere; here we learn from John that it must also be *effective*:

> "If a man who was rich enough in this world's goods saw that one of his brothers was in need, but closed his heart to him, how could the love of God be living in him? My children, our love is not to be just words or mere talk, but something real and active" (1 Jn 3:17-18).

We find the same teaching expressed in a more colourful way in the Letter of James:

> "If one of the brothers or sisters is in need of clothes and has not enough food to live on, and one of you says to them, 'I wish you

well; keep yourself warm and eat plenty', without giving them these bare necessities of life, then what good is that?" (Jas 2:15-16)

In the primitive community of Jerusalem this need translated into sharing. Of the first Christians it is said that "they sold their goods and possessions and shared out the proceeds among themselves according to what each one needed" (Acts 2:45). They were driven to this not by an ideal of poverty, but of charity; the aim was not for everyone to be poor, but so that among them there would be no one "ever in want" (Acts 4:34). The need to translate love into concrete gestures of charity was not strange to the apostle Paul as well, who, as we have seen, insists so much on the love of the heart. This is shown by the importance he gives to the collections for the poor (2 Cor 8-9).

On this matter the apostolic Church has simply brought together the teaching and example of the Master, whose compassion for the poor, the sick and the hungry never remained just an empty sentiment, but was always translated into concrete help, and who made these concrete gestures of charity part of the final judgement (cf. Mt 25).

Church historians see in this spirit of fraternal solidarity one of the main factors of the "mission and expansion of Christianity in the first three centuries".[32] It translated into special initiatives – and later into institutions – for the care of the sick, support to widows and orphans, help to prisoners, meals for the poor, assistance for strangers. The second part of Pope Benedict XVI's Encyclical *Deus caritas est*, and, institutionally, the Pontifical Council's *Cor Unum*, is about this aspect of Christian charity, in history and today.

## 2. The emergence of the social problem

The modern era, especially the 19th century, signalled a turning point in this, bringing the social problem to the fore. It was noticed that it was not sufficient to provide for the needs of the poor and the oppressed on a case-by-case basis, but it was necessary to act on the structures which create the poor and oppressed. That it was new territory, at least thematically, can be deduced from the very title and opening words of Leo XIII's Encyclical *Rerum Novarum* of 15 May 1891, with which the Church entered into the debate as a protagonist. It is worth re-reading the start of the Encyclical:

---

[32] A von Harnack, *Mission und Ausbreitung des Christentums in den ersten drei Jahrhunderten*, Leipzig 1902.

"That the spirit of revolutionary change, which has long been disturbing the nations of the world, should have passed beyond the sphere of politics and made its influence felt in the cognate sphere of practical economics is not surprising. The elements of the conflict now raging are unmistakable, in the vast expansion of industrial pursuits and the marvellous discoveries of science; in the changed relations between masters and workmen; in the enormous fortunes of some few individuals, and the utter poverty of the masses; the increased self-reliance and closer mutual combination of the working classes; as also, finally, in the prevailing moral degeneracy".

Into this order of problems should be placed the second Encyclical of Pope Benedict XVI on charity: *Caritas in veritate.* I am no expert in this field and so I will refrain from entering into the merits of the content of this and other social encyclicals. What I would like to do is to illustrate the historical and theological background, the so-called *Sitz im Leben,* of this new form of ecclesiastical magisterium; that is, how and why social encyclicals began to be written and new ones periodically appear. This in fact can help us to discover something new about the gospel and Christian love. Saint Gregory the Great says "Sacred Scripture grows with those who read it" *(Scriptura cum legentibus crescit)*,[33] that is it always reveals new meanings according to the questions put to it, and this is shown to be particularly true in the present topic.

Mine will be a summary "bird's eye" reconstruction, so to speak, which can be done in a few minutes, but syntheses and summaries also have their use, especially when, due to a variety of tasks, one is unable personally to study a certain problem in depth.

At the time when Leo XIII wrote his social encyclical, there were three dominant trends about the social significance of the gospel. First of all there was the social and Marxist interpretation. Marx was not concerned about Christianity from this perspective, but some of his immediate followers (Engels still from an ideological point of view and Karl Kautsky from an historical point of view) examined the problem, in the field of research into the "precursors of modern socialism".

The conclusions they reached were as follows. The gospel was principally a major social proclamation addressed to the poor;

---

33 Saint Gregory the Great, *Commentary on Job*, XX, 1 (CCL 143, pg. 1003).

everything else, its religious application, was secondary, a "superstructure". Jesus was a great social reformer, who wanted to redeem the lower classes from poverty. His programme foresaw the equality of all people, the freeing from economic need. That of the primitive Christian community was an *ante litteram* Communism, still somewhat naïve in character, not scientific: a Communism in consumption more than the production of goods.

Subsequently, the historiographers of the Soviet regime rejected this interpretation which, in their opinion, conceded too much to Christianity. In the 1960s the revolutionary interpretation re-appeared, this time in more political than economic tones, with the idea of Jesus as the head of a "zealot" liberation movement, but it was short-lived and at this time lies outside our field.

A similar conclusion to the Marxist one, but with a different aim, was reached by Nietzsche. For him, too, Christianity was born as a counter-movement of the lower classes, but the judgement of this was totally negative. The gospel incarnates resentment of the weak against the powerful forces; it is the "inversion of all values", a clipping of the wings of humanity's aspiration towards greatness. All that Jesus intended to do was to spread throughout the world, in opposition to earthly misery, a "kingdom of heaven".

Alongside these two schools – in agreement in the way of seeing things but in opposition to the judgements made – is a third which we can call conservative. According to this school, Jesus was not at all interested in social and economic problems; to attribute these concerns to him would be to diminish him, secularise him. He drew images from the world of work and the needy and poor were close to his heart, but he never aimed at improving the living conditions of people in their earthly lives.

## 3. Theological reflection:
## Liberal and dialectical theology

These were the dominant ideas in the culture of the time, when, on the part of the Christian Churches, theological reflection began, too, about the problem. This also developed in three stages and offers three trends: that of liberal theology, that of dialectical theology and that of the Catholic Magisterium.

The first response was that of the *liberal theology* of the end of the 19th and start of the 20th century, represented in this field above all by Ernst Troeltsch and Adolph von Harnack. It is worth focussing a little on the ideas of this school because many of the conclusions it reached, at least in this specific area, are those which, by another route, the Church's social magisterium also reached and which are still current and sustainable.

Troeltsch questioned the starting point of the Marxist interpretation, according to which the religious element is always secondary compared to the economic one, a simple superstructure. Studying Protestant ethics and the start of capitalism, he showed that, if the economic element influences the religious one, it is also true that the religious influences the economic. They are two distinct spheres, not subordinated one to the other.

Harnack, for his part, noticed that the gospel does not provide us with a direct social programme to combat and abolish need and poverty, it does not express judgements about the organisation of labour, and other aspects of life important for us today, such as art and science. And he notes how lucky that is! Woe betide us if it had done otherwise and tried to give rules about relations between the classes, working conditions, and so on.

In order to be concrete, such rules would have been fatally tied to the conditions of the world then (as are many institutions and social precepts of the Old Testament), and so subsequently would have been anachronistic and even a "useless encumbrance" for the gospel. History, even that of Christianity, shows how dangerous it is to be tied to social structures and political institutions of a certain era and how difficult it is then to be free of them. But let us see what Harnack says:

> "No religion...ever went to work with such an energetic social message, and so strongly identified itself with that message as we see to be the case in the Gospel. How so? Because the words "Love thy neighbour as thyself" were spoken in deep earnest; because with these words Jesus turned a light upon all the concrete relations of life, upon the world of hunger, poverty and misery...Its object is to transform the socialism which rests on the basis of conflicting interests into the socialism which rests on the consciousness of a spiritual unity...The fallacious principle of the free play of forces, of the "live and let live" principle – a better name for it would be the "live and let die" – is entirely opposed to the Gospel".[34]

---

34 A von Harnack, *Das Wesen des Cristentums*, Leipzig 1900; English translation *What is Christianity?*, London, Williams and Norgate, 1904.

The position of the evangelical message is opposed, as can be seen, both to the reduction of the gospel to a social proclamation and class struggle, and to the position of the economic liberalism of the free play of the forces. At times the Protestant theologian gives into a certain enthusiasm:

> "A new spectacle presented itself to the world; up to then religion was either to do with things of the world, adapting itself easily to the status quo, or it was camped out in the clouds, putting itself in direct opposition to everything. Now, instead, a new duty to be carried out presented itself, to hold as of little value the need and misery of this earth, and similarly earthly prosperity, while relieving poverty and need of every kind; to raise up one's head to heaven with the courage which comes from faith, and to work with the heart, the hands and the voice for the brethren in this world".[35]

What criticism did *dialectical theology*, which succeeded liberal theology after the First World War, have of this liberal vision? Above all its starting point, its idea of the kingdom of

---

[35] A von Harnack, *Il cristianesimo e la società*, Mendrisio 1911, pgs. 12-15.

heaven. For the liberals it was of an essentially ethical nature; a sublime moral ideal, which has its roots in the paternity of God and the infinite value of every soul; for the dialectical theologians Karl Barth, Rudolph Bultmann and Martin Dibelius, it is of an eschatological nature; it is a sovereign and gratuitous intervention of God, who does not aim at changing the world, but denouncing its current structure ("radical critique"), announcing its imminent end ("consequent eschatology"), launching an appeal for conversion ("radical imperative").

The gospel's topicality lies in the fact that "its demands are not made in a general way, to everyone and for all time, but to this person, and perhaps only to this person, at this moment and perhaps only at this moment; and the demand is not based on an ethical principle, but on the situation in which God has placed that person, and perhaps only that person, requiring a decision from that person here and now".[36] The gospel's influence in social matters happens through the individual, not through the community or ecclesial institution.

---

36 M Dibelius, *Das soziale Motiv im Neuen Testament*, in *Botschaft und Geschichte*, Tubingen 1953, pgs. 178-203.

Today, the challenge for the believer in Christ comes from the situation created by the industrial revolution with the changes which it brought to the rhythm of life and work, with the consequent disregard for the human person. In the face of this, "Christian" solutions are not provided, each believer is called to respond to it under their own responsibility, in obedience to the call which reaches him/her from God in the concrete situation in which they live, although the fundamental criterion is found in the precept of love of neighbour. The human person must not resign him or herself pessimistically before situations, but nor must they have any illusions about changing the world.

In this perspective, can one still speak about a social significance of the gospel? Yes, but only of method, not content. Let me explain. This vision reduces the social significance of the gospel to a "formal" significance, excluding any "real" significance, or content. In other words, the gospel provides the method, or the impulse, for a correct Christian attitude and action in the social sphere, nothing else.

Here is the weakness of this vision. Why attribute to the gospel accounts and parables simply a formal significance ("How do I welcome the call to decision which comes to me, here and now?") and not a real and exemplary significance, too? Is it lawful, for example, with regard to the parable of the rich man Dives, to ignore the concrete and clear indications contained there about the use and abuse of wealth, luxury, contempt for the poor, to stick just to the "imperative of the hour" which sounds throughout the parable? Wouldn't it be strange, at least, if Jesus intended to say simply that there, before him, it was necessary to decide for God and that, to say this, he had set up such a complex and detailed tale which would distract attention from, rather than focus on the centre of interest?

Such a solution, which strips the flesh from the message of Christ, moves from the erroneous presupposition that there are no common demands in the word of God which apply for the rich today, as they did for the rich – and the poor – at the time of Jesus. Almost that the decisions asked for by God were something empty and abstract – purely making a decision – and not deciding about something. All the parables with a social background are called "parables of the kingdom" and thereby their content is levelled out simply into eschatological significance.

## 4. The Church's social doctrine

The social doctrine of the Catholic Church, as always, seeks synthesis rather than contrast, the method of *et-et* (both-and) rather than *aut-aut* (either-or). It maintains the "dual enlightenment" of the gospel: the eschatological and the moral. In other words: it is in agreement with dialectical theology on the fact that the kingdom of God preached by Christ is not essentially ethical in nature, that is, an ideal which draws its strength from the universal validity and perfection of its principles, but it is a new and gratuitous initiative of God which, in Christ, breaks in from on high.

It departs from the dialectical vision, however, in the way of conceiving the relationship between this kingdom of God and the world. There is no opposition and incompatibility between the two, just as there is no opposition between the work of creation and that of redemption and, as we saw in the first meditation, just as there is no opposition between agape and eros. Jesus compared the kingdom of God to the yeast added to the dough to make it rise, to the seed thrown on the earth, to the salt which gives flavour to food; he said he came not to judge the world, but to save the world. This allows us to see the influence of the gospel in the social sphere in a different and much more positive light.

However, despite all the differences in approach, there are some common conclusions which emerge from the whole theological reflection on the relationship between the gospel and social issues. We can summarise them in this way. The gospel does not provide direct solutions to social problems (as we have seen, woe betide us if it had attempted to do so!): however it contains principles which lend themselves to drawing up concrete responses to different historical situations. Since the social situations and problems change from era to era, the Christian is called to incarnate from time to time the principles of the gospel in the situation of the moment.

This is precisely the contribution of the papal social encyclicals. So they follow on from each other, each one taking up the matter again from the point where the previous ones left off (in the case of Benedict XVI's encyclical, it follows on from Paul VI's *Populorum progressio*) and updates it on the basis of new demands emerging in society (in this case, the phenomenon of globalisation) and also on the basis of an ever new examination of the word of God.

The title of Benedict XVI's social encyclical, *Caritas in veritate*, indicates what are for him the biblical foundations on which he intends to base the discourse on the social significance of the gospel: charity and truth. He writes:

"Truth preserves and expresses charity's power to liberate in the ever-changing events of history. It is at the same time the truth of faith and of reason, both in the distinction and also in the convergence of those two cognitive fields. Development, social well-being and the search for a satisfactory solution to the grave socio-economic problems besetting humanity, all need this truth. What they need even more is that this truth should be loved and demonstrated. Without truth, without trust and love for what is true, there is no social conscience and responsibility, and social action ends up serving private interests and the logic of power, resulting in social fragmentation, especially in a globalized society at difficult times like the present".[37]

The difference lies not just in what is said and the solutions proposed, but also in the genre adopted and the authority of the proposal. It consists, in other words, in the passage from free theological discussion to the magisterium and from an intervention in social issues of an exclusively "individual" nature (like that proposed by dialectical theology) to a

---

[37] Benedict XVI, *Caritas in veritate*, no. 5.

communal intervention, as Church and not just as individuals.

## 5. To serve, and not be served

Let us conclude with a practical matter which affects everyone, even those among us who are not called to work directly in social issues. We have seen Nietzsche's idea about the social significance of the gospel. For him, yes, it was the fruit of a revolution, but a negative revolution, a regression compared to Greek culture; it was the revenge of the weak against the strong. One of the points he picked on was the preference given to service over dominance, to making oneself small over wanting to put oneself forward and aspire to great things.

He accused Christianity for one of the most beautiful gifts it has given to the world. One of the principles by which the gospel chiefly and most beneficially influences the social sphere is in fact precisely that of service. It is no accident that it occupies an important place in the social doctrine of the Church. Jesus made service one of the cornerstones of his teaching; he himself said that he had come to serve and not to be served:

"Anyone who wants to become great among you must be your servant, and anyone who wants to be first among you must be slave to all. For the Son of Man himself did not come to be served but to serve, and to give his life as a ransom for many" (Mk 10:43-44).

It is enough to reflect on these words of Jesus to understand the error of Nietzsche's interpretation. "If anyone wants to be great among you": so aspiring to greatness, wanting to realise magnanimous things in life is not forbidden, only the way to achieve greatness has changed. It is not that of the superman who raises himself over others, sacrificing them if necessary for his own gain, but it is that of lowering oneself, thus raising one's own life and that of others.

Service is a universal principle; it applies to every aspect of life: the state should be at the service of the citizens, politics at the service of the state, the doctor at the service of the sick, the teacher at the service of students. In itself, it is not a virtue (in no list of virtues, or fruits of the Spirit, in the New testament is *diakonia* mentioned), but it flows out from different virtues, especially from humility and charity. It is a way for that love which "does not seek [its] own interests but thinks of other people's interests instead" (Phil 2:4) to manifest itself, that love which gives without seeking in return.

Evangelical service, as opposed to that of the world, is not proper to the inferior person, the needy, but rather the superior, the one who is on high. Jesus says that, in his Church, it is above all "the leader" who must be "as if he were the one who serves" (Lk 22:26), the first must be "slave to all" (Mk 10:44). In his book *Gift and Mystery*, John Paul II expresses this significance of the authority in the Church with a strong image. They are some verses composed by him in Rome at the time of the Council:

> "Peter, you are the floor, on which others may walk to arrive there wherein you guide their steps – as a rock endures the noisy hoofing of a herd".

Let us end by listening to the words which Jesus said to his disciples immediately after having washed their feet, as if they were addressed to us here and now:

> "'Do you understand' he said 'what I have done to you? You call me Master and Lord, and rightly; so I am. If I, then, the Lord and Master, have washed your feet, you should wash each other's feet. I have given you an example so that you may copy what I have done to you'" (Jn 13:13-15).

# V

# HE LOVED US WHEN WE WERE ENEMIES: GOOD FRIDAY HOMILY

IN HIS passion, writes St Paul to Timothy, Jesus Christ "spoke up as a witness" (1 Tim 6:13). We ask ourselves: witness to what? Not to the truth of his life and his cause. Many people have died, and still die today, for a mistaken cause, believing it to be right. Now, the resurrection certainly does testify to the truth of Christ: "And God has publicly proved this by raising this man [Jesus] from the dead", the Apostle was to say in the Areopagus at Athens (Acts 17:31).

Death does not testify to the truth of Christ, but to his love. In fact, it is the supreme proof of that love. "A man can have no greater love than to lay down his life for his friends" (Jn 15:13). One could object that there is a greater love than giving your life for your friends, and that is to give your life for your enemies. But this is precisely what Jesus did: "Christ died for sinful men", the Apostle writes in the Letter to the Romans. "It is not easy to die even for a good man – though of course for someone really worthy, a man might be prepared to die – but what proves that God loves us is that Christ died for us while we were still sinners" (Rom 5:6-8). "He loved us as enemies, that we might be made friends".[38]

A certain one-sided "theology of the cross" can make us forget what is essential. The cross is not just God's judgement on the world, refutation of its wisdom and revelation of its sin. It is not God's "no" to the world, but his "yes" of love. "Injustice, evil as a reality", writes Pope Benedict XVI in his book on Jesus, "cannot simply be ignored, left alone. It must be dealt with, it must be overcome. This is true mercy. And now, since men are unable to, God himself does it – this is God's unconditional goodness".[39]

\* \* \*

How can we have the courage to speak about God's love, while every day before our eyes

---

[38] Saint Augustine, *Homilies on the First Epistle of John*, 9, 9 (PL 35, 2051).

[39] Cf. J Ratzinger – Benedict XVI, op. cit., pg. 133.

there are images of misfortune and tragedies, the latest being the terrible catastrophe which struck Japan with the earthquake on 11 March 2011? Should we not speak about it at all? But to remain in total silence would be to betray the faith and ignore the meaning of the mystery we are celebrating.

There is a truth to be proclaimed strongly on Good Friday. The one whom we contemplate in the cross is God "in person". Yes, it is also the man Jesus of Nazareth, but that man is one person with the Son of the eternal Father. As long as the fundamental dogma of the Christian faith is not recognised and taken seriously – the first dogma defined at Nicaea – that Jesus Christ is the Son of God, God himself, of one substance with the Father, then, human suffering will remain unanswered.

One cannot say that "Job's question has remained unanswered" and that not even the Christian faith has an answer to give to human suffering, if one starts by rejecting the answer it does claim to have. What do you do to reassure someone that a particular drink does not contain poison? You drink it yourself first, in front of him. This is what God has done for humanity. He has drunk the bitter cup of the passion. So, human suffering cannot be a poisoned chalice, it cannot be just negativity, loss, absurd, if God himself has chosen to taste it. At the bottom of the chalice there must be a pearl.

We know the name of that pearl: resurrection! "I think that what we suffer in this life can never be compared to the glory, as yet unrevealed, which is waiting for us" (Rom 8:18), and again: "He will wipe away all tears from their eyes; there will be no more death, and no more mourning or sadness. The world of the past has gone" (Rev 21:4).

If life's race ended in this world, we would have every reason to despair at the thought of the millions and perhaps billions of human beings who start off at a great disadvantage, nailed to the starting line by poverty and underdevelopment, while a few grant themselves every luxury and do not know how to spend the disproportionate amounts they earn.

But it is not so. Death not only cancels out differences, but overturns them. "Now the poor man died and was carried away by the angels to the bosom of Abraham. The rich man also died and was buried. In his torment in Hades..." (cf. Lk 16:22-23). We cannot apply this scheme of things to the social sphere in a simplistic way, but it is there to warn us that faith in the resurrection lets no-one go on living their own quiet life. It reminds us that the saying "live and let live" must never turn into "live and let die".

The response of the cross is not just for us Christians, it is for everyone, because the Son of God died for all. In the mystery of the redemption, there is an objective and a subjective aspect; there is the fact itself, and then awareness of the fact and the response of faith to it. The first extends beyond the second. "The Holy Spirit", says a Vatican II text, "offers to all the possibility of being made partners, in a way known to God, in the paschal mystery".[40]

One of the ways of being associated with the paschal mystery is precisely that of suffering. "To suffer", wrote John Paul II following the attempt on his life and the subsequent lengthy convalescence, "means to become particularly susceptible, particularly open to the working of the salvific powers of God, offered to humanity in Christ".[41] Suffering, all suffering, but especially that of the innocent, brings us into contact in a mysterious way, "known only to God", with the cross of Christ.

\* \* \*

After Jesus, those who have "spoken up as a witness" and who "have drunk from the

---

40 *Gaudium et spes*, no. 22.

41 *Salvifici doloris*, no. 23.

chalice" are the martyrs! Initially, the accounts of their death were called *"passio"*, passion, like that of the sufferings of Jesus. Once again, the Christian world has been visited by the ordeal of martyrdom which was thought to have ended with the fall of totalitarian atheistic regimes. We cannot pass over their testimony in silence. The first Christians honoured their martyrs; the acts of their martyrdom were read and circulated among the Churches with tremendous respect.

There is something which distinguishes the authentic accounts of martyrdom from legendary ones, constructed theoretically after the end of the persecutions. In the former, there is almost no trace of arguments against the persecutors; all attention is focussed on the heroism of the martyrs, not on the perversity of the judges and the slaughter. Saint Cyprian even ordered his followers to give twenty-five gold coins to the executioner who beheaded him. These are disciples of the one who died saying: "Father, forgive them, for they do not know what they are doing". "The blood of purification [of Jesus] pleads more insistently than Abel's" (Heb 12:24): it does not call for vendetta and punishment, but it is reconciliation".[42]

---

42 J Ratzinger – Benedict XVI, op. cit., pg. 187.

Even the world bows before modern witnesses of faith. This explains the unexpected success in France of the film 'Of Gods and Men', which tells the story of the seven Cistercian monks slain in Tibhirine in March 1996. And who can fail to admire the words written in his will by Shahbaz Bhatti, a Catholic politician in Pakistan who was killed for his faith in March 2011? His testament is a legacy to us, his brothers and sisters in the faith, and it would be an act of ingratitude to allow it to be quickly forgotten. He wrote:

> "I was offered high government positions and asked to quit my struggle but I always refused to give up, even at the cost of my life. I do not want popularity; I do not want any position. I just want a place at Jesus' feet. I want my life, my character, my actions to speak for me and indicate that I am following Jesus Christ. Because of this desire, I will consider myself most fortunate if – in this effort and struggle to help the needy and the poor, to help the persecuted and victimised Christians of Pakistan – Jesus Christ will accept the sacrifice of my life. I want to live for Christ and I want to die for Him".

We seem to hear again the martyr Ignatius of Antioch, when he went to Rome to suffer martyrdom. The silence of the victims, however, does not justify the guilty indifference of the world before their fate. "The upright perish", lamented the prophet Isaiah, "and no one cares. Devout men are taken off and no one gives it a thought" (Is 57:1).

\* \* \*

Christian martyrs are not the only ones, as we have seen, to suffer and die around us. What can we believers offer to those who have no faith, apart from the certainty our own faith gives us that there is a ransom for suffering? We can suffer with those who suffer, weep with those who weep (cf. Rom 12:15). Before proclaiming the resurrection and the life, in front of the weeping sisters of Lazarus, "Jesus wept" (Jn 11:35). At this time we can suffer and weep, especially with the Japanese people, now recovering from one of the most terrible natural disasters in history. We can also say to these brothers and sisters in humanity that we admire the example of dignity and composure they have given to the world.

Globalisation at least has this positive effect: the suffering of one people becomes the suffering of all, arouses the solidarity of all. It gives us the opportunity to discover that we are one single human family, joined together for good or ill. It helps us overcome all barriers of race, colour and creed. As one of our poets put it: "Peace, you peoples! Too deep the mystery of the prostrate earth".[43]

But we must also take in the teaching contained in such events as these. Earthquakes, hurricanes and other disasters which strike the innocent and the guilty alike are never punishments from God. To say otherwise would be to offend both God and humanity. But they do contain a warning: in this case, a warning against the danger of deluding ourselves that science and technology will be enough to save us. Unless we practice some restraint in this field, we see that they themselves can become, and we are seeing it, the greatest threat of all.

There was also an earthquake at the moment Christ died: "Meanwhile the centurion, together with the others guarding Jesus, had seen the earthquake and all that was taking place, and they were terrified and said, 'In truth this was a son of God'" (Mt 27:54). But there was an even "greater" one at the moment of his resurrection: "And all at once there was a violent earthquake, for the angel of the Lord, descending from

---

43 G Pascoli, *I due fanciulli.*

heaven, came and rolled away the stone and sat on it" (Mt 28:2). This is how it will always be. Every earthquake that brings death will always be followed by an earthquake of resurrection and life.

Someone once said: "Only a god can save us now".[44] We have the sure and certain guarantee that he will do it because "God loved the world so much that he gave his only Son" (Jn 3:16). Once upon a time the rainbow was the sign of the covenant between God and humanity, now it is the cross, and it is a new and eternal covenant. Let us, then, prepare to sing the words of the liturgy with new conviction and heartfelt gratitude: *"Ecce lignum crucis, in quo salus mundi pependit:* This is the wood of the cross, on which hung the Saviour of the world". *"Venite, adoremus:* Come, let us worship".

---

44 *Antwort. Martin Heidegger im Gespräch,* Pfullingen 1988 ("Nur noch ein Gott kann uns retten").